The Best of
Wild Rice
Recipes

Beatrice Ojakangas

Published by
Adventure Publications
P.O. Box 269
Cambridge, MN 55008
1-800-678-7006
ISBN: 0-934860-56-4

Salads and Dressings

Side Dishes

Main Dishes

Crepes, Waffles and Bread

Desserts

"How-To"

HOW TO COOK WILD RICE ON THE RANGE TOP

2 cups cooked rice

2/3 c. wild rice
1/2 to 1 tsp. salt
2-1/2 c. water

Wash wild rice in three changes of hot tap water; drain. In saucepan, heat rice, salt and water to boiling. Reduce heat and cover. Simmer until rice is tender and has absorbed the water, this will take from 30 to 45 minutes. Drain at the 30-minute mark for chewier rice. Rice should be tender but not "rolled back" or mushy. Some kernels will be open, but others will be just tender.

HOW TO COOK WILD RICE IN THE OVEN

2 cups cooked rice

2/3 c. wild rice
1/2 to 1 tsp. salt
2-1/2 c. water

Wash wild rice in three changes of hot water; drain. Combine rice, water and salt in ovenproof casserole; cover. Bake at 325° for one hour to one hour and 20 minutes. This method works well when you are roasting poultry or meat along with the rice. If desired, you can add other ingredients such as onions, celery, mushrooms or other vegetables to the rice before baking.

Cook wild rice using this method if you already have another part of the meal in the oven.

HOW TO COOK WILD RICE IN THE MICROWAVE OVEN

2 cups cooked rice

2/3 c. wild rice
1/2 to 1 tsp. salt
2-1/2 c. water

Wash wild rice in three changes of hot water; drain. Combine rice, water and salt in an uncovered 2-quart glass bowl or casserole. Microwave on HIGH for five minutes or until mixture boils; reduce power to MEDIUM and cook for 30 to 35 minutes. Let stand 10-15 minutes; drain if there is excess water.

Wild rice takes just as long to cook in the microwave as on the range top, but the microwave takes less energy and is a convenience, especially in the summertime.

HOW TO "POP" WILD RICE

Be forewarned: Not all wild rice will "pop" successfully. The best rice to use is hand-processed wild rice that usually has more moisture left in each kernel, which will expand when heated.

Place 1/2" oil in a small, shallow pan with a small strainer set in the oil. Heat at high temperature until oil is about 450°. Drop one kernel of rice into the strainer. When it sizzles, cracks open and expands to about double its length, the oil is ready. (You may wish to reduce the heat temporarily.) Add one tablespoon rice at a time to the oil. When all kernels have expanded (which constitutes the "popping"), dump out onto paper toweling. Repeat, adjusting heat as necessary. Crisp popped rice may be seasoned with salt, pepper and mixed herbs. Or you may use as a garnish on salads, soups and casseroles.

Appetizers

CURRIED WILD RICE APPETIZERS

15 appetizers

1 c. cooked wild rice
1 3-ounce pkg. cream cheese
1 green onion, sliced
1 tsp. curry powder

Dash cayenne
1/3 c. chopped chutney
Chopped pecans
Chopped parsley
Toasted sesame seeds

Blend wild rice into the cream cheese along with the onion, curry powder and cayenne. Blend in the chutney. Shape into balls the size of small walnuts. Roll in chopped nuts, parsley or sesame seeds. Chill until firm.

WILD RICE STUFFED EGGS

24 appetizers

1/4 c. raw wild rice
1-1/2 tsp. caraway seeds
2 c. water
12 hard-cooked eggs, peeled
  and halved

4 slices bacon, cooked,
  crumbled
6 Tbsp. mayonnaise
2 Tbsp. Dijon-style mustard
Salt and pepper to taste

Combine wild rice, caraway seeds and water; simmer uncovered until water is absorbed and rice is cooked. Mash the egg yolks and stir in the cooked wild rice, bacon, mayonnaise, mustard, salt and pepper to taste. Fill egg white halves with yolk mixture. Chill until ready to serve.

BAKED WILD RICE AND CHEESE BALLS

24 appetizers

1/4 c. raw wild rice
1 5-oz. jar cheddar cheese
  spread

1 c. all-purpose flour
1/2 tsp. baking powder
1/2 stick soft butter

Cook wild rice according to directions on page 8. In large bowl of electric mixer, blend together the cheese spread, flour, baking powder and butter. Blend in drained wild rice. Shape into 1" balls. Chill until firm. (Make several days ahead if desired.) Arrange on lightly greased cookie sheet. Bake at 350° 12-15 minutes until puffed and lightly browned.

Soups

WILD RICE AND PECAN SOUP

6 to 8 servings

2/3 c. raw wild rice
1 c. coarsely chopped pecans
1/2 c. butter
2 Tbsp. chopped green onion
1 clove garlic, pressed
8 c. beef broth
2 Tbsp. tomato paste

2 Tbsp. cornstarch
3 Tbsp. water
1 Tbsp. dry Sherry
1 egg yolk
1/4 c. heavy cream
Salt, white pepper and nutmeg
  to taste

Wash wild rice in three changes of hot tap water, drain and set aside. In heavy 4-quart pot, sauté rice for 10 minutes until toasted. Add beef broth and tomato paste. Bring to a boil. Cook 35-45 minutes until wild rice is done. Mix cornstarch, water and sherry. Stir into the boiling mixture. Cook, stirring, until thickened. Blend egg yolk with cream. Whisk into the soup; do not boil. Taste, season. Add pecans to soup.

GAZPACHO WITH WILD RICE

6 tomatoes, peeled, seeded
 and chopped; save juice
Tomato juice, canned
2 cucumbers, peeled, seeded
 and chopped
2 cloves garlic, minced
1/2 c. chopped green pepper

1/2 c. chopped onion
3 eggs
1/3 c. olive oil
1/2 c. red wine vinegar
1/8 tsp. red pepper flakes
Salt and pepper to taste
Cooked wild rice

Strain juice from tomatoes into measuring cup; add canned tomato juice to equal two cups. Combine tomatoes, cucumbers, garlic, green pepper and onion. In food processor blend eggs, oil, vinegar and red pepper. Turn on food processor, add tomato juice. Process until pale red and emulsified. Pour sauce over tomato mixture. Season to taste. Chill at least 4 hours or overnight. To serve, ladle soup into bowls and top with cooked wild rice.

WILD RICE SPINACH SOUP

6 servings

2/3 c. raw wild rice
4 c. chicken broth
1 c. finely-chopped onion
1 small clove garlic, crushed
2 Tbsp. butter or oil
2 10-1/2 oz. pkgs. frozen chopped spinach

1/2 c. light cream
1 tsp. curry powder
1 tsp. salt
1/4 tsp. pepper
Thinly sliced lemon

Wash wild rice in three changes of hot tap water; drain. Place rice and 2-1/2 cups chicken broth in saucepan. Bring to a boil and simmer 35-40 minutes or until rice is cooked. Meanwhile, sauté onions and garlic in oil in a 2-quart saucepan until tender. Add remaining chicken broth and spinach; simmer until spinach is cooked; 10 minutes. Puree in blender until smooth. Return to saucepan and add cream, curry, salt, pepper and cooked wild rice including any unabsorbed broth. Serve with a twist of lemon.

CREAMY WILD RICE MUSHROOM SOUP

6 servings

1/2 c. raw wild rice
1-1/2 c. water
2 green onions, thinly sliced
1/2 lb. mushrooms, sliced

3 Tbsp. butter
1/4 c. flour
4 c. chicken broth
1 c. cream
2 Tbsp. sherry

Wash wild rice in three changes of hot tap water; add to water in saucepan, heat to boiling, cover and lower heat; simmer 35-45 minutes. Sauté onions and mushrooms in butter until onion is transparent, 3-5 minutes. Add flour and stir, cooking for 5 minutes. Stir in chicken broth and bring to a boil; stir until smooth and flour is thoroughly cooked. Add wild rice, cream and sherry, stirring until heated through.

WILD RICE VEGETABLE SOUP

6 servings

1/2 c. raw wild rice, rinsed
2 c. boiling chicken broth
1 lb. mushrooms, sliced
4 Tbsp. butter

1/2 c. each onion, celery and
green pepper, chopped
1/2 c. all-purpose flour
8 c. chicken broth

Cook wild rice in broth over low heat for 30-35 minutes or until wild rice is tender. Remove from heat, cover; do not drain. In large saucepan, sauté mushrooms in 2 Tbsp. of butter 10 minutes. Remove from pan, reserve. Add remaining butter to saucepan; sauté onion, celery and green pepper until tender. Puree mixture in blender or food processor, adding a little chicken stock if necessary. Return to pan with all but 1/2 c. of the chicken broth; return to a boil. Blend flour with reserved chicken stock to make a paste; stir into boiling mixture and cook until thickened. Add mushrooms and wild rice; taste and add salt and pepper. Keep hot until ready to serve.

SMOKEY WILD RICE SOUP

6 servings

1/2 c. raw wild rice
3 slices smoked bacon, diced
1/2 c. each chopped onion,
 celery and carrot

5 c. chicken broth
1 c. whipping cream
1/4 tsp. salt
1/4 tsp. white pepper
Parsley for garnish

Rinse rice in three changes of hot tap water; drain. In heavy pot, cook bacon until crisp; add onion, celery, carrot and rice. Cook, stirring occasionally, until onions are translucent, three minutes. Add the chicken broth; heat to a boil. Reduce heat to low, cover and simmer until rice is tender, 45 minutes to an hour. Add the cream and season with salt and pepper. Sprinkle with parsley.

CHICKEN, WILD RICE BROCCOLI SOUP

8 servings

2 c. raw wild rice
3 Tbsp. butter
1 onion, chopped
1/2 lb. fresh mushrooms, chopped
2 lbs. broccoli, chopped

3 carrots, finely chopped
2 c. chicken broth
2 Tbsp. flour
2 c. light cream
2 c. cooked, diced chicken
Salt and pepper to taste

Cook rice according to directions on page 8. In heavy pot, melt the butter; add the onion and mushrooms. Sauté for 5 minutes or until vegetables are cooked. Add the broccoli, carrots and chicken broth. Simmer until vegetables are tender. Turn vegetables into a blender or food processor and process until smooth. Add the flour and cream; blend until smooth. Return to pot. Heat to simmering and cook until thickened. Add the chicken and wild rice. Add salt and pepper to taste.

Salads

WILD RICE AND BROCCOLI SALAD

8 servings

1 c. raw wild rice
2 Tbsp. beef bouillon granules
1/4 lb. turkey ham, cut julienne
1/4 lb. pepper cheese, julienne
3/4 c. broccoli florets
4 green onions, thinly sliced
1 carrot shredded
3/4 c. walnut halves

Dressing:
2 Tbsp. lemon juice
2 Tbsp. white wine vinegar
1/2 tsp. dry mustard
1/2 to 1 tsp. curry powder
1/2 c. olive oil
Salt and pepper
Lettuce leaves

Cook wild rice with bouillon as directed on page 8; drain. In a bowl, combine rice with ham, cheese, broccoli, onions, carrot and walnut halves. In a small bowl, whisk together the dressing ingredients, adding curry powder, salt and pepper to taste. Toss with wild rice mixture and serve over lettuce if desired.

CURRIED WILD RICE SALAD

6 servings

2/3 c. raw wild rice
4 green onions, sliced
  including tops
12 stuffed green olives,
  sliced

1 4-oz. jar marinated artichoke
  hearts, quartered
1-1/2 tsp. curry powder
1/2 c. mayonnaise
1/4 c. chopped parsley

Cook wild rice according to directions on page 8; drain and cool. In large bowl, combine the wild rice with onions, olives and artichoke hearts. Mix together curry powder and mayonnaise, add to the wild rice mixture. Serve immediately, or cover and chill until serving time. Before serving, garnish with chopped parsley.

WILD RICE GREEN BEAN SALAD

6 servings

2/3 c. raw wild rice
1 lb. tender fresh green beans
Boiling water
1 3"-piece fresh ginger, pared, chopped
3 Tbsp. sherry vinegar or white wine

1 tsp. sesame oil
1/2 tsp. coarse salt
1/4 tsp. sugar
1/8 tsp. white pepper
1/3 c. olive oil
4 Tbsp. toasted sesame seeds

Cook wild rice according to directions on page 8. Trim beans and cut on the diagonal, 1/4" thick. Drop into boiling water, cook three minutes. Drain, rinse immediately under cold running water. Process gingerroot and vinegar in blender until pureed, drain; save liquid, discard pulp. Whisk sesame oil, salt, sugar and pepper into ginger-liquid. Whisk in oil until blended. Blend with the beans and rice. Toss to blend. Chill. Top with sesame seeds.

WILD RICE AND ASPARAGUS SALAD

6 servings

2/3 c. raw wild rice
1 lb. tender fresh asparagus
Boiling water
1 3"-piece fresh ginger,
  chopped
3 Tbsp. (sherry) wine vinegar

1 tsp. sesame oil
1 tsp. salt
1/4 tsp. sugar
1/8 tsp. white pepper
1/3 c. olive oil
4 Tbsp. toasted sesame seeds

Cook wild rice as directed on page 8; drain and cool. Trim asparagus, but leave in whole spears; cook in boiling water three minutes. Drain; rinse under cold running water. Process ginger and vinegar in blender until pureed. Strain into a bowl, whisk in sesame oil, salt, sugar, pepper and olive oil until blended. Pour dressing on asparagus; drain off most of it. Blend remainder into wild rice. Arrange asparagus on top of the wild rice in serving dish. Sprinkle with sesame seeds. Chill or serve at room temperature.

WILD RICE CHICKEN SALAD

6 servings

2/3 c. raw wild rice
Red Pepper Vinaigrette
 (see next recipe)
2 c. cooked chicken, cubed
1 c. diced celery *and/or*
1 pkg. frozen artichoke hearts,
 cooked

1/2 c. chopped parsley
1/2 c. sliced green onion
2 tsp. tarragon leaves
Lettuce and tomato wedges
Toasted slivered almonds,
 pistachios or pine nuts

Cook wild rice as directed on page 8; drain and cool. Prepare the Red Pepper Vinaigrette. Combine cooked, cooled rice with the chicken, celery, artichokes (if used), parsley, green onion and tarragon. Mix in the Red Pepper Vinaigrette. Line serving bowl or platter with tomato wedges, turn rice mixture into center and sprinkle with nuts for garnish.

RED PEPPER VINAIGRETTE

One cup

2 Tbsp. Dijon-style mustard
3 Tbsp. white wine vinegar
1 tsp. salt

1/2 tsp. ground black pepper
1/4 tsp. crushed red pepper
flakes
3/4 c. olive oil or safflower oil

Put mustard, vinegar, salt, black and red pepper into bowl. Whisk in the oil to make a smooth, thickened dressing.

WILD RICE CHICK-PEA SHRIMP SALAD

8 servings

2/3 c. raw wild rice
1 tsp. thyme leaves
12 oz. large cooked shrimp
1 16-oz. can garbanzo beans
  or chick peas*

1 6-oz. can pitted black olives
1 sweet red onion, thinly sliced
1 2-oz. jar sliced pimento
Crisp lettuce
Lemon Vinaigrette

Cook wild rice as directed on page 8, adding thyme to cooking water; drain and cool. In a large bowl, combine the cooked and cooled wild rice, shrimp, garbanzo beans, olives, onion and drained pimento. Pile into individual lettuce cups or serve in lettuce-lined salad bowl. Drizzle with the Lemon Vinaigrette.

* *Chick peas* and *garbanzo beans* are two names for the same thing!

LEMON VINAIGRETTE

About 2/3 cup

4 Tbsp. fresh lemon juice
1 Tbsp. Dijon-style mustard
1 tsp. dill weed

1 tsp. chervil
1/3 c. olive oil or safflower oil
Salt and freshly-ground pepper

In a small bowl, whisk together lemon juice, mustard, dill weed and chervil. Whisk in the oil until blended. Add salt and pepper to taste.

CHICKEN MELON SALAD ON WILD RICE   10 to 12 servings

1-1/3 c. raw wild rice
2 c. chicken broth
6 boneless chicken breast
  halves, skinned
2 red bell peppers, halved
  and cored

1/2 c. toasted slivered almonds
1 10-oz. pkg. frozen whole
  kernel corn, thawed
1/2 c. grapefruit, segmented
1/2 honeydew melon, sliced thin
  with peel removed
3 Tbsp. minced parsley

Cook wild rice according to directions on page 8. Simmer broth and chicken in saucepan until chicken is done. Place red peppers skin side up on a cookie sheet; roast at 550° for 10 minutes or skin blisters. Cover, cool; peel, cut into strips. Slice chicken diagonally. Turn wild rice onto serving platter and top with the chicken, vegetables and fruit. Garnish with the pepper strips. Sprinkle with parsley. Serve with Curry Mayonnaise, next page.

CURRY MAYONNAISE

Two cups

3 shallots, minced
3 Tbsp. Dijon-style mustard
4 Tbsp. fresh lime juice
1 egg yolk

1 Tbsp. curry powder
3/4 c. oil: half olive oil,
 half safflower oil
1/4 c. sour cream
1 Tbsp. chopped chives

Whisk together shallots, mustard, lime juice, egg yolk and curry powder. Whisk in oil until mixture is thick. Fold in sour cream and chives.

WILD RICE SALAD WITH HERBS

6 servings

2/3 c. raw wild rice
1/3 c. fresh lemon juice
1/8 tsp. freshly-ground pepper
2/3 c. olive oil
1/2 c. thin sliced green onion

1/2 c. chopped parsley
1/3 c. chopped fresh mint
Crisp romaine leaves
1 medium tomato, seeded and
  chopped
Alfalfa sprouts

Cook wild rice according to directions on page 8. Mix cooked rice with the lemon juice, pepper, olive oil, green onion, parsley and mint leaves. Cover and refrigerate at least 2 hours for flavors to blend. Serve over a bed of romaine; garnish with chopped tomato and alfalfa sprouts.

PITA BREAD SANDWICHES

Stuff *Wild Rice Salad with Herbs* into split pocket or pita breads. Garnish with shredded cheese and additional vegetables and sunflower seeds.

WILD RICE, CHICKEN PASTA SALAD

8 to 10 servings

2/3 c. raw wild rice
6 boneless chicken breasts,
  about 1-1/2 lbs.
1/2 c. chicken stock
1/2 c. pine nuts or slivered
  almonds
1 lb. of your favorite pasta,
  cooked al dente

2 c. uncooked chick peas
2 6-oz. jars artichoke hearts
1 10-oz. pkg. frozen peas
1 lb. mushrooms, sliced
1 c. sliced stuffed olives
1 c. sliced black olives
1 red bell pepper, sliced
Herb Dressing, see next page

Cook wild rice as directed on page 8; drain. Put chicken breasts bone-side down in a skillet or shallow pan. Add chicken stock. Cover; simmer 25 minutes. Cool in the stock. Drain. Cut into strips. Mix wild rice, nuts, chicken, pasta, chick peas, artichoke hearts, peas, mushrooms, olives and peppers; toss to blend. Prepare the dressing and blend into the salad.

HERB DRESSING

About 3/4 cup

2-3 Tbsp. red wine vinegar
1/4 c. fresh parsley, minced
2 tsp. Dijon-style mustard

1/2 tsp. curry powder
1/2 c. olive oil
Salt and freshly-ground pepper

In a mixing bowl, whisk together the vinegar, parsley, mustard and curry powder. Whisk in the oil until dressing is blended. Taste and add salt and pepper.

WILD RICE AND AVOCADO SALAD

4 servings

2/3 c. raw wild rice
1 tsp. Dijon-style mustard
1/2 tsp. salt
1-1/2 tsp. sugar
3 Tbsp. Balsamic or
 cider vinegar

1/3 c. olive oil
2 green onions, minced
 with tops
2 avocados, peeled and diced
1/2 red bell pepper, thinly sliced
 for garnish

Cook wild rice as directed on page 8; drain and cool. Meanwhile, whisk together mustard, salt, sugar and vinegar. Slowly whisk in the oil until blended. Add the green onions and avocado cubes. In large bowl, fold together cooled rice with the dressing, onions and avocados. Serve chilled or at room temperature garnished with thinly sliced red bell pepper, if desired.

WILD RICE SEAFOOD SALAD

4 to 6 servings

2/3 c. uncooked wild rice
1/3 c. mayonnaise
1/3 c. sour cream
1/4 c. tomato-based chili sauce
1 Tbsp. lemon juice
1 tsp. Dijon-style mustard
1/2 c. thinly sliced green onion

1 tomato, peeled, diced
1 c. thinly slice celery
1/2 lb. cooked crabmeat
Salt and pepper to taste
Lettuce
Chopped parsley
Hard-cooked eggs, sliced

Cook wild rice according to directions on page 8; drain and cool. In large bowl, blend together mayonnaise, sour cream, chili sauce, lemon juice and mustard. Turn into serving bowl and refrigerate. Combine wild rice, onion, tomato, celery and crabmeat; fold together gently until blended. Add salt and pepper. Serve wild rice mixture in individual lettuce cups. Garnish with parsley and/or hard-cooked eggs. Pour dressing on salad at the table.

WILD RICE ARTICHOKE MUSHROOM SALAD 4 to 6 servings

2 c. cooked wild rice	1/4 lb. fresh mushrooms, sliced
1/3 c. golden raisins	1 Tbsp. fresh chives, minced
2/3 c. frozen green peas	Basil Vinaigrette (next page)
1 c. diced turkey ham	Watercress, Bibb lettuce,
1 6-oz. can marinated artichoke	or garden lettuce
hearts, drained	Fresh parsley for garnish

Wild rice should be cold and dry. In salad bowl, combine rice with the raisins, peas, turkey ham, artichoke hearts, mushrooms, and chives. Prepare *Basil Vinaigrette* and fold into the wild rice mixture. Refrigerate one to two hours. Toss again. Arrange on watercress or lettuce and garnish with parsley.

BASIL VINAIGRETTE

About 1/2 cup

1 Tbsp. white wine vinegar
1 Ibsp. Dijon-style mustard
1 tsp. basil leaves
1/2 tsp. salt

1/2 tsp. freshly-ground black
   pepper
4 Tbsp. olive oil, or combination
   of olive oil and peanut oil

Measure vinegar, mustard, basil, salt and pepper into bowl. Slowly whisk in the oil until mixture is smooth and emulsified.

WILD RICE "HEALTH" SALAD

4 to 6 servings

2 c. cooked wild rice
8 eggs, hard-cooked, chopped
1/3 c. wheat germ
1 cup crisp bean sprouts
1 green pepper, chopped

2 green onions, sliced with tops
1 tomato, seeded, diced
Salt and pepper to taste
Yogurt Dressing (next page)
Crisp greens

In a bowl, toss the rice with the eggs, wheat germ, bean sprouts, green pepper, onion and tomato. Add salt and pepper to taste. Prepare *Yogurt Dressing* and blend into mixture. Serve on crisp greens.

This salad is also good spooned into pita breads to make sandwiches.

YOGURT DRESSING

One cup

1 c. unflavored lowfat yogurt
1 tsp. Dijon-style mustard

1/4 tsp. salt
1 tsp. Italian-style herb blend

Blend yogurt with the mustard, salt and herb blend. Let stand 30 minutes for flavors to blend.

Side Dishes

WILD RICE, TOMATOES, HERBS ON NOODLES 6 servings

2/3 c. raw wild rice
3 med. tomatoes, peeled,
  seeded and diced
4 cloves garlic, minced
1/2 c. chopped fresh parsley
1/2 c. chopped fresh basil *or*
  2 Tbsp. dried basil leaves
1/2 tsp. freshly-ground pepper

1 Tbsp. fresh mint leaves
  chopped
Salt to taste
1/4 tsp. hot pepper flakes
1/2 c. olive oil
1 10-oz. pkg. spinach noodles
1/2 c. grated Parmesan
2 c. shredded fontina cheese

Cook wild rice as directed on page 8. In medium bowl, mix rice with tomatoes, garlic, parsley, basil, pepper, mint, salt, peppers and olive oil. Let stand at room temperature 30 minutes to 4 hours for flavors to blend. Cook noodles as directed to "al dente;" blend in cheeses while still warm. Turn into a large, shallow bowl; top with rice mixture. Serve at room temperature.

WILD RICE CORN PUDDING

8 servings

1/3 c. raw wild rice
1-1/2 c. whole kernel corn
3 eggs, well-beaten
2 Tbsp. fresh onion, minced
1/4 c. flour
1-1/2 tsp. salt

1/4 tsp. white pepper
1 Tbsp. sugar
Dash nutmeg
2 Tbsp. melted butter
2 c. light cream
1 jar pimentos, chopped

Cook wild rice as directed on page 8. In large bowl, combine the cooked wild rice, corn, eggs and onion; mix well. Combine flour, salt, pepper, sugar and nutmeg. Stir into corn mixture. Add butter, cream, and pimentos; mix well. Pour into buttered 2-quart shallow baking dish. Set dish in a larger pan and pour hot water to 1" depth around dish. Bake at 325°, uncovered, for one hour or until pudding is firm and knife inserted in center comes out clean. Cut into squares; serve hot.

RATATOUILLE WITH WILD RICE

12 to 16 servings

2/3 c. raw wild rice
3/4 c. olive oil or salad oil
2 med. green peppers, sliced
1/2 lb. mushrooms, sliced
1 c. thinly-sliced onion
2 cloves garlic, minced

3 med. zucchini, 1/4" slices
1 small eggplant, 1/2" dices
4 tomatoes, peeled, wedged
2 tsp. salt
1/4 tsp. pepper
1/4 c. chopped fresh parsley

Cook wild rice as directed on page 8. Heat 1/4 c. oil in skillet or wok. Add green peppers, mushrooms, onion and garlic. Sauté 5 minutes. Remove to large bowl. Sauté zucchini in 2 Tbsp. oil on high heat 10 minutes until tender. Put into bowl with vegetables. Sauté eggplant and remaining oil 5 minutes over high heat. Return all vegetables to skillet. Toss in cooked wild rice and half the tomato wedges. Season and sprinkle with parsley. Top with remaining tomato wedges. Serve hot or at room temperature.

SPICY EGGPLANT CUBES AND WILD RICE   4 to 6 servings

2/3 c. raw wild rice
1 medium eggplant,
 about 1-1/2 lbs.
1 medium onion, cut in 1/2"
 slices

2 tsp. curry powder
1/4 tsp. powdered ginger
6 Tbsp. peanut oil
1/2 tsp. salt
2 tsp. fresh lemon juice
2 Tbsp. mango chutney

Cook wild rice as directed on page 8. Cut eggplant into 1" cubes and turn into a bowl. Add the onion, curry powder and ginger. Toss to mix. In deep skillet or wok, heat the oil over high heat. Add eggplant and sauté, tossing frequently, for about 3 minutes. Reduce high heat to medium and cook, tossing frequently, until eggplant is tender and browned, about 25 minutes. Add the salt, lemon juice and chutney; fold in the wild rice. Serve hot, chilled or at room temperature.

WILD RICE WITH GREEN ONIONS

6 servings

1 c. raw wild rice	1 Tbsp. butter
3 green onions, sliced, including green part	2-3/4 c. chicken broth
	1 tsp. salt

Wash wild rice in three changes of hot tap water; drain well. In saucepan, sauté the green onions in the butter over medium heat until soft, about two minutes. Add the wild rice, chicken broth and salt. Bring to a boil. Reduce heat to low. Cover and simmer 45 minutes until rice is tender and broth is absorbed. Serve hot.

WILD RICE LYONNAISE

6 servings

1 c. sliced onions
2 Tbsp. butter or vegetable oil
1 2-oz. jar sliced pimentos

3 c. cooked wild rice *or*
  1-1/2 c. each wild and brown
  rice
1/2 tsp. dried tarragon
  (optional)

Sauté onions in the butter over low heat for 15 minutes or until golden. Add the pimentos, rice and tarragon. Cook over low heat until rice is heated through, stirring occasionally. Serve warm.

WILD RICE SLOW BAKED WITH SWEET ONION, BARLEY AND BROWN RICE

6 servings

1/3 c. each: wild rice, pearl barley and brown rice
2 Tbsp. butter
1 clove garlic, minced
1/2 lb. sliced mushrooms

1 large sweet onion, sliced into 1/4" rings
3 c. beef or chicken broth
1 tsp. thyme
Salt and pepper to taste

Wash wild rice in three changes of hot tap water. Combine drained rice with the barley and rice. In heavy 2-quart casserole, heat butter and add garlic; sauté for one minute. Add the grains and sauté for 2-3 minutes until shiny, stirring. Add mushrooms, onions, broth and thyme. Bake along with a meat or poultry, covered. At 300°, the casserole bakes for 2-1/2 hours. At 350°, it is done in one hour. Add salt and pepper to taste.

WILD RICE WITH BROWN RICE

Three cups

1/2 c. wild rice, washed	2-1/2 c. water
1/2 c. brown rice	1 tsp. salt

Wash wild rice in three changes of hot tap water; drain well. Combine with the brown rice, water and salt in a 2-quart saucepan. Bring to a boil, cover and simmer 35-40 minutes until rices have absorbed the liquid and are tender. Cooking time varies a little with the type of brown rice you use and the wild rice.

Note: Because wild rice and brown rice cook in approximately the same length of time, they can be cooked successfully together.

WILD RICE WITH LENTILS

4 servings

1/2 c. raw wild rice
1/2 c. lentils
2 Tbsp. clarified butter
1 large sweet onion, sliced thin

3 c. boiling water
1-1/2 tsp. salt
1 to 3 tsp. Garam Masala or
    curry powder

Wash rice and lentils in three changes of hot tap water. Heat butter in heavy frying pan. Add the onions and sauté 3 to 4 minutes until golden brown. Remove half the fried onions and reserve. Add rice and lentils to pan and sauté, stirring continuously for 3 minutes. Add hot water, salt and garam masala or curry powder. Bring to a boil, cover and simmer over very low heat for 30-35 minutes or until rice and lentils are cooked. Do not lift lid or stir during cooking. Serve hot, garnished with the reserved fried onion.

WILD RICE WITH PEARL BARLEY

4 servings

1/2 c. raw wild rice
2 Tbsp. butter
1 large sweet onion, sliced thin
1/2 c. pearled barley

3 c. boiling water
1-1/2 tsp. salt
1/4 tsp. freshly-ground pepper
1/4 tsp. allspice

Wash wild rice in three changes of hot tap water; drain. Heat butter in heavy skillet and add the onions. Sauté 3 to 4 minutes until golden brown. Remove half the fried onions and reserve. Add rice and barley to pan. Sauté, stirring, for 3 minutes. Add hot water, salt, pepper and allspice. Heat to boiling. Cover and simmer over very low heat for 30-35 minutes or until rice and barley are cooked. Do not lift lid or stir during cooking. Serve hot, garnished with the reserved fried onion.

MUSHROOM RICE

1 c. sliced onions
1/2 lb. mushrooms, sliced
3 Tbsp. chopped fresh parsley
3 Tbsp. vegetable oil

3 c. cooked wild rice *or*
  1-1/2 c. each wild *and* brown
  rice
1/4 c. wheat germ
1/2 tsp. basil
1/2 tsp. cumin seeds

Sauté onions, mushrooms and parsley in the oil for five minutes over medium heat. Add remaining ingredients; heat through, stirring constantly. Serve hot.

WILD RICE ALMONDINE

6 servings

2/3 c. raw wild rice
4 Tbsp. butter

1 c. slivered or sliced almonds
Salt and pepper to taste

Cook wild rice according to directions on page 8. In a large skillet, melt the butter; add the almonds and cook over medium to low heat until almonds are toasted. Blend in the wild rice and add salt and pepper to taste.

WILD RICE AND PEA PODS

2/3 c. raw wild rice
4 Tbsp. butter

1/2 lb. fresh edible pea pods,
trimmed
Salt, pepper and dill weed

Cook wild rice according to directions on page 8. In a skillet or wok, melt the butter and add the pea pods. Stir-fry over high heat until pea pods are bright green, 2-3 minutes. Add the wild rice; season with salt, pepper and dill weed to taste. Serve hot.

WILD RICE AND JICAMA

2/3 c. raw wild rice	Salt and pepper to taste
1 bulb jicama root, about 1 lb.	Fresh coriander or cilantro
4 Tbsp. butter	to taste

Cook wild rice according to directions on page 8. Peel the jicama and cut into julienne sticks (about 1/8" x 2"). In large skillet or wok, melt the butter. Add the jicama and stir-fry over high heat until heated through. Add the wild rice, salt and pepper. Turn into a serving dish and sprinkle with chopped fresh coriander or cilantro.

WILD RICE PILAF

4 servings

2/3 c. raw wild rice
4 Tbsp. butter

1/2 c. pine nuts or slivered
    almonds
1/4 c. coarsely-chopped
    pistachios

Cook wild rice according to directions on page 8. In heavy skillet, melt the butter. Add the pine nuts or almonds and pistachios. Stir over medium heat until nuts are toasted, about 5 minutes. Add the wild rice and stir until heated through. Serve warm.

WILD RICE AND SPINACH FRITTATA

6 servings

3 Tbsp. olive oil
1/2 c. thinly sliced green onion
10 eggs
1 c. cooked wild rice
1 c. fresh spinach, chopped fine

1/3 c. grated Parmesan cheese
1 Tbsp. chopped fresh parsley
1 clove garlic, minced
1 tsp. salt
1/4 tsp. pepper

Heat oil in a heavy 10"-skillet. Add onion and sauté until onion is tender, about 5 minutes. In large bowl, combine remaining ingredients. With wire whisk, beat until blended. Turn into skillet with onion. Cook over low heat for three minutes, lifting from bottom with spatula as eggs set. Bake uncovered at 350° for 10 minutes or until top is set. With spatula, loosen from bottom and around edges; slide onto serving platter. Cut into wedges.

WILD RICE, CARROTS, MUSHROOMS

6 to 8 servings

2/3 c. raw wild rice	1/4 lb. mushrooms, diced
2-1/2 c. chicken broth	1/2 tsp. thyme leaves
6 slices smokey bacon, diced	1/2 tsp. marjoram leaves
1 med onion, coarsely-chopped	1/4 tsp. black pepper
2 small carrots, diced to 1/4"	1-1/2 Tbsp. butter

Wash wild rice in three changes of hot tap water. Turn into a 2-quart casserole and cover with the boiling chicken broth. Set aside. In a heavy skillet, cook the bacon until crisp; remove bacon and drain. Spoon out all but 3 Tbsp. of the fat. Add onion, carrots, mushrooms, thyme, marjoram and pepper. Sauté 4 minutes, stirring, until vegetables are almost cooked. Turn into casserole with the wild rice. Stir. Cover. Bake at 350° for 2 hours or until rice is cooked. Stir in the butter. Top with bacon.

WILD RICE, BACON AND MUSHROOMS

4 servings

2/3 c. raw wild rice
1-1/2 tsp. salt
4 slices bacon

1/3 c. chopped onion
1/3 c. chopped mushrooms
1/2 tsp. freshly-ground black
pepper

Cook wild rice according to directions on page 8 using 1 tsp. of the salt; drain well. In heavy skillet, fry bacon until crisp. Add the onion and mushrooms and cook, stirring 3 to 4 minutes until they begin to brown. Add wild rice, stir until mixed. Add remaining 1/2 tsp. salt and pepper.

APPLE RAISIN WILD RICE PILAF

6 servings

1 c. raw wild rice, rinsed in
  hot water
3 c. apple cider
6 Tbsp. butter
1/2 c. sliced almonds
1/2 c. raisins

3/4 tsp. salt
1/2 tsp. pepper
1/2 tsp. cinnamon
1/4 tsp. nutmeg
1 large apple: pared, cored
  and diced

In a large saucepan, combine the wild rice with cider and 1-1/2 cups water. Heat to boiling, stir, cover and simmer 40-45 minutes until rice is cooked. Drain. In heavy skillet, melt butter; add the almonds and raisins and cook over medium heat until almonds are toasted, stirring. Add remaining ingredients and sauté two minutes. Stir in the cooked wild rice. Heat to serving temperature.

HOT WILD RICE AND CRANBERRY RELISH

6 servings

1-1/3 c. raw wild rice
1 10-oz. package frozen cranberries with orange relish, thawed

Cook wild rice as directed on page 8, using double the amounts of water and salt. Combine the rice and thawed cranberry relish in a buttered 2-quart casserole. Cover and bake at 350° for 20-30 minutes or until heated through.

Note: This is great served with your holiday turkey or ham.

WILD RICE, CRANBERRY MUSHROOM STUFFING

6 servings

2/3 c. raw wild rice
3 Tbsp. butter
1-1/2 c. chopped mushrooms
1/2 c. chopped onion

1/4 tsp. salt
Freshly-ground pepper
1 c. chopped fresh cranberries
1/3 c. currants or raisins

Cook wild rice according to directions on page 8. You should have about two cups cooked rice. In skillet, heat butter and add mushrooms and onions; sauté until mushrooms are cooked and dry and onions are soft, about 10 minutes on medium to low heat. Add remaining ingredients and wild rice. Makes about three cups stuffing, enough for six double-thick pork chops or six boneless chicken breasts or six chicken legs. Place stuffing into meat, fasten. Bake, broil or barbecue until meat is cooked. Use this stuffing also for roast chicken or turkey.

FRUITED WILD RICE STUFFING

6 cups stuffing

1 c. raw wild rice
3-1/2 c. water
1 c. bread crumbs
1/2 c. raisins

1/2 c. chopped walnuts
1 apple, pared and chopped
1/2 c. butter, melted
1/4 c. orange juice

Cook wild rice, as directed on page 8, using 1 cup rice and 3-1/2 cups water. Combine cooked, drained rice with all of the remaining ingredients. Use as stuffing for game birds, turkey, capon or chicken, or turn into buttered 2-quart casserole and bake at 325° for 1-1/2 hours, covered.

Note: This makes enough stuffing for a 10-lb. turkey. You may also use it as a base for baked chicken or turkey breast, or to fill boned and pounded chicken breasts.

CARROT, RAISIN WILD RICE STUFFING

3 cups stuffing

1/2 c. raw wild rice	6 green onions, sliced
1-1/2 c. water	1 apple, cored and chopped
1/4 c. butter	2 Tbsp. lemon juice
1 c. shredded carrots	1/2 tsp. fresh ground cardamom
1/2 c. golden raisins	1/2 tsp. salt
1/2 c. chopped slivered almonds	Pepper

Cook wild rice, as directed on page 8, using 1/2 c. rice and 1-1/2 cups water. Melt butter in sauté pan and add carrots, raisins, almonds, onion, apple and lemon juice. Cook over medium heat until carrots are done, about five minutes. Remove from heat; stir in rice. Add cardamom, salt and pepper. Use stuffing for chicken, turkey and other poultry dishes.

Main Dishes

PORK CHOP WILD RICE CASSEROLE

4 servings

2/3 c. raw wild rice
1 14-1/2 oz. can chicken broth
1/4 c. white wine or apple cider
1 large onion, chopped

4 pork chops, cut 1" thick
1 small tart apple, cored, sliced
1 medium tomato, sliced
Chopped fresh parsley

Wash rice in three changes of hot tap water. Turn into a 2-quart casserole. Add the broth, wine and onion. Arrange chops over the top. Cover and bake at 325° for one hour. Uncover and top chops with a slice of apple and a slice of tomato. Recover and continue baking for 30 minutes longer.

WILD RICE QUICHE

6 servings

1 10"-round or 9x12" tart pan with partially-baked pie shell	2 Tbsp. butter
1/2 lb. turkey ham, diced 1/4"	3 green onions, minced
2 c. shredded Swiss cheese	1/2 green pepper, diced
1 c. cooked wild rice	4 eggs
	1 c. heavy cream

Prepare the pie shell using your favorite recipe. Sprinkle ham, cheese and wild rice into pie shell. In small frying pan, melt butter; add onion and green pepper and cook over medium high heat until onion is soft, 3-4 minutes. Sprinkle mixture over the ham, cheese and wild rice. Beat together eggs and cream. Pour over mixture in pie shell. Bake in a preheated 375° oven for 35-45 minutes or until quiche is set. Serve hot or cooled.

WILD RICE STUFFED TURKEY BREAST

Stuffing:
2/3 c. wild rice
1/4 c. butter
1 c. shredded carrots
1/2 c. golden raisins
1/2 c. chopped pistachios, pine
 nuts or slivered almonds
6 green onions, sliced
1 apple, cored, finely chopped
2 Tbsp. lime juice
1/2 tsp. fresh-ground cardamom
1/2 tsp. each salt and pepper

Turkey and sauce:
1 boneless turkey breast,
 about 3 lbs.
2 Tbsp. melted butter
1/2 c. dry white wine
2 tsp. juniper berries
1/3 tsp. thyme leaves
1 c. heavy cream
1 Tbsp. Calvados or brandy

(Continued on next page)

Cook wild rice according to directions on page 8. Melt butter in sauté pan and add carrots, raisins, nuts, onion, apple and lime juice. Cook over medium-high until carrots are done. Remove from heat; stir in rice. Add cardamom, salt and pepper. Put turkey breast between sheets of plastic wrap; with flat side of mallet, pound into a 12x14x1" rectangle. Spoon stuffing lengthwise down center of the turkey breast. Pull meat up around filling to enclose it, pressing firmly into a roll. Tie in several places or use the "bookbinders" wrap. Brush with melted butter. Place stuffed turkey in baking pan. Preheat oven to 325°. Combine wine, juniper berries and thyme. Pour over meat. Roast 45 minutes to one hour until thermometer inserted in the center of the roll reads 165-170°. Remove strings; keep turkey warm. Degrease pan, add cream and spoon out the juniper berries. Bring liquids to a boil and cook over medium-high heat until reduced by half and thickened. Stir in Calvados. To serve, place turkey on heated platter. Spoon extra stuffing on one side. Spoon sauce over the turkey to glaze; serve the remaining sauce on the side.

STIR FRY WILD RICE, SNOW PEAS, PORK

4 servings

2/3 c. raw wild rice	1/2 lb. snow peas, trimmed
1/2 lb. pork tender, 1/4" slices	1 Tbsp. grated fresh ginger
3 Tbsp. peanut oil	1 Tbsp. cornstarch
1 c. sliced celery	1 Tbsp. dry sherry
1 c. sliced green onion	3 Tbsp. soy sauce
1 c. sliced fresh mushrooms	1/2 tsp. salt (optional)
1 can sliced water chestnuts	1/2 c. cashews

Cook wild rice according to directions on page 8. Heat oil in heavy skillet; add sliced pork and stir-fry over high heat for 2 minutes until meat is no longer pink. Add celery, green onion, mushrooms, water chestnuts, pea pods and ginger. Stir-fry for 5 minutes over high heat until vegetables are tender-crisp; add wild rice. Mix cornstarch with sherry, soy sauce and salt; add to pan juices and cook until thickened. Toss together to coat with glaze.

SCAMPI ON WILD RICE WITH GARLIC BUTTER 8 servings

2/3 c. raw wild rice
2 lbs. large green shrimp
1/2 c. butter
1 tsp. salt

6 cloves garlic, minced
1/4 c. chopped fresh parsley
2 tsp. grated lemon peel
2 Tbsp. lemon juice
Lemon wedges

Cook wild rice according to directions on page 8. Remove shells from shrimp, leaving shell on tail section only. Devein; wash and dry. Melt butter in 9x13" baking dish in oven as you preheat it to 400°. Add salt, garlic and parsley; mix well. Arrange shrimp in single layer in baking dish, turn over to butter both sides of shrimp. Bake uncovered for 5 minutes. Turn shrimp; sprinkle with lemon peel, lemon juice and remaining parsley. Bake 8-10 minutes, or just until tender. Arrange hot wild rice onto serving dishes. Arrange shrimp on top. Garnish with lemon wedges.

WILD RICE BUFFET CASSEROLE

6 servings

2/3 c. raw wild rice
1/4 c. olive oil
1 large onion, chopped
1/4 lb. mushrooms, quartered

1 16-oz. can tomatoes and juice
1 c. halved pitted ripe olives
1 c. shredded cheddar cheese
Salt and pepper to taste

Cook wild rice according to directions on page 8. In a heavy skillet, heat the oil. Add the onion; cook 2 minutes until transparent. Add the fresh mushrooms, tomatoes (including juices) and olives. Combine with the cooked rice. Fold in the cheese and add salt and pepper to taste. Turn into a 1-1/2-quart casserole. Cover and refrigerate, if desired, up to 24 hours. Or bake immediately at 375° for 30 minutes or until heated through. Baking time will be longer if dish has been refrigerated.

WILD RICE AND EGGS BRUNCH CASSEROLE   8 servings

2/3 c. raw wild rice
1/4 c. butter
1 c. fresh mushrooms, sliced
1/2 c. red bell pepper, chopped
3 Tbsp. flour

1 tsp. salt
1/4 tsp. white pepper
2 c. light cream
1 c. shredded Swiss cheese
8 eggs

Cook wild rice according to directions on page 8. Melt butter in a skillet; add mushrooms and pepper; cook 3-4 minutes. Add flour, salt and pepper. Stir in cream and cook until mixture thickens. Add the cheese. Add half the sauce to the wild rice. Spread into a buttered, shallow 2-quart casserole. Make 8 indentations. Put a spoonful of the sauce into each indentation. Crack one egg into each. Drizzle on remaining sauce. Bake at 350° for 20 to 25 minutes until eggs are cooked.

SHRIMP AND WILD RICE

6 to 8 servings

1-1/3 c. raw wild rice
1/4 c. olive oil
1/2 tsp. dried oregano
1 clove garlic, minced
1 tsp. salt

Freshly-ground black pepper
2 tsp. lemon juice (to taste)
6 Tbsp. dry white wine
24 large raw shrimp, peeled
4 Tbsp. butter, melted

Cook wild rice according to directions on page 8 (use 5 cups water); drain. Add oil, oregano, garlic, salt, pepper, lemon juice and wine to the rice. Turn into a 1-1/2 quart shallow baking dish. Bake uncovered, at 350° for 30 minutes, stirring 2 or 3 times. Heat butter in skillet and add the shrimp; toss until cooked and hot. Turn shrimp onto wild rice mixture. Bake 10 minutes longer, uncovered. Serve warm.

HERBED CHICKEN AND WILD RICE CASSEROLE

6 servings

2/3 c. raw wild rice
1 small onion, chopped
1 clove garlic, minced
2 Tbsp. oil
1 stalk celery, chopped
1/2 c. chopped green pepper
1/2 c. sliced fresh mushrooms
2 c. cooked, chopped chicken
 or turkey

3 c. chicken broth
1/4 tsp. basil
1 Tbsp. parsley flakes
1/4 tsp. sage
1/8 tsp. pepper
1/2 c. sliced water chestnuts
1/2 c. slivered almonds
3 Tbsp. chopped pimento
1/2 to 1 c. dairy sour cream

Cook wild rice, see page 8. Put oil in heavy skillet, sauté onion and garlic 2 minutes. Add celery, green pepper, mushrooms, chicken, broth, basil, parsley, sage and pepper. Blend in rice. Add remaining ingredients, blend. Cover and bake in a 2-1/2 quart casserole 45 minutes until bubbly.

WILD RICE AND CHICKEN BREASTS

6 servings

1-1/3 c. raw wild rice
1 Tbsp. olive oil or butter
6 boneless chicken breasts,
  skinned

1 c. heavy cream
2 Tbsp. sun-dried tomatoes,
  chopped
1 Tbsp. fresh basil leaves,
  chopped

Cook wild rice according to directions on page 8 using 5 cups water. Season with salt and pepper. Turn into a shallow buttered casserole. Heat oil in heavy skillet, add chicken breasts and sauté over medium to low heat just until cooked through. Remove chicken breasts and place on wild rice in casserole. Add cream to pan and bring to a boil, scraping in all the brownings. Add tomatoes, salt and pepper to taste. Pour sauce over chicken. Cover and bake at 350° just until heated through, 20-30 minutes, longer if made ahead and refrigerated. Sprinkle with basil; serve hot.

Crepes, Waffles
and Breads

HERBED WILD RICE CREPES

15 to 16 5"-crepes

3 eggs
1-1/2 c. cold milk
3/4 c. cold water
1/4 tsp. salt

1 c. all-purpose flour
1/2 c. cooked wild rice
1 tsp. thyme
Butter for cooking crepes

In a bowl, whisk together the eggs, milk, water, salt, flour, wild rice and thyme. Let rest for 30 minutes. Heat crepe pan until a drop of water sizzles on the surface. Lightly butter pan. Make crepes using 1/3 c. batter at a time. Stack on a piece of waxed paper as crepes are done. Fill with seafood, meat, poultry or other favorites. See following recipe for *Party Mushroom Crepes.*

PARTY MUSHROOM CREPES

12 herbed crepes, page 84
2/3 c. raw wild rice
3 lbs. fresh mushrooms, chopped
2 Tbsp. butter
1 large onion, chopped
2 cloves garlic, minced

1/4 c. all-purpose flour
3/4 c. light cream
2 Tbsp. dry sherry, optional
1/2 c. grated Parmesan cheese
1/4 c. chopped parsley
Salt and pepper to taste
Sour cream for serving

Cook wild rice, see page 8. In a heavy skillet, sauté mushrooms in butter; add onions and garlic and cook until moisture disappears, about 10 minutes. Add flour; cook 2 minutes. Add cream and sherry; stir and cook 5 minutes until thickened. Add rice, Parmesan and parsley; taste and season if needed. Divide filling between crepes; roll up. Place into shallow pan. Brush with butter, broil until lightly browned. Serve with sour cream.

WILD RICE CREPES

Makes about 15 5" crepes

3 eggs
1/2 c. cold milk
3/4 c. cold water
1/4 tsp. salt

1 c. all-purpose flour
1/2 c. cooked wild rice,
  see page 8
Butter for cooking crepes

In a bowl, whisk together the eggs, milk, water, salt, flour and wild rice. Let rest 30 minutes. Heat crepe pan until a drop of water sizzles on the surface. Lightly butter pan. Make crepes using 1/3 c. batter at a time. Stack crepes on a piece of waxed paper as they are done.

WILD RICE CREPES WITH BERRIES AND CREAM

Wild rice crepes, page 86
Lingonberry preserves *or:*

Fresh raspberries, blueberries
  or strawberries
Plenty of whipped cream

Spread each crepe with one to two tablespoons of lingonberry preserves or 1/4 c. fresh raspberries, blueberries or strawberries. Top with a rounded spoonful of whipped cream. Roll up and serve with additional whipped cream.

NORTH COUNTRY WILD RICE PANCAKES

16 pancakes

4 eggs	1 tsp. sugar
1-1/4 c. buttermilk	1/2 tsp. salt
1/2 tsp. baking soda	2 Tbsp. melted butter
1-1/4 c. all-purpose flour	1 c. cooked wild rice,
1 tsp. baking powder	see page 8

In large bowl, whisk together the eggs, buttermilk and baking soda. Whisk together flour, baking powder, salt and sugar; add to the egg mixture. Whisk in melted butter and wild rice. Cook pancakes on hot, greased griddle until golden on both sides. Serve with butter and warm fruit or maple syrup.

Note: For thicker pancakes, use only 2 eggs.

WILD RICE AND BLUEBERRY MUFFINS

12 muffins

1-1/2 c. all-purpose flour	1/4 c. melted butter
1/2 c. sugar	2 eggs
2 tsp. baking powder	1/2 c. milk
1 tsp. ground coriander	1 c. fresh blueberries*
1/2 tsp. salt	1/2 c. cooked wild rice

In a bowl, stir together the flour, sugar, baking powder, coriander and salt. In another bowl, whisk together butter, eggs and milk. Sprinkle a tablespoon of dry ingredients over blueberries and roll them around to coat with flour mixture. Fold the liquid ingredients into the dry. Then fold in the coated blueberries and the wild rice. Batter will be rather stiff. Spoon into 12 well-buttered muffin tins. Bake in a preheated 400° oven 15-20 minutes.

*Note: You can use frozen, unsugared whole blueberries, partially thawed.

KITCHI GUMI FRY BREAD

Makes 4 rounds

2 c. all-purpose flour
1 Tbsp. baking powder
3/4 tsp. salt
1/2 c. cornmeal

1 c. cooked wild rice,
  see page 8
1 c. water or milk
Oil for frying

In a large bowl, blend flour, baking powder, salt, 1/4 c. of the cornmeal and wild rice. Stir in water or milk until dough is stiff. Divide into four parts; knead each part slightly until dough is smooth. Sprinkle board with remaining cornmeal and roll each part out to about 10" diameter, the size of the frying pan. Heat oil in pan to smoking-hot, about 400°. Fry one bread at a time for 45 seconds to one minute on each side, just until golden. Remove to paper toweling. Repeat for each remaining bread. Best served hot, dusted with powdered sugar. Cut or tear into wedges. This is a quick bread that is fried in a shallow pan of oil, typical of Indian fry breads.

WILD RICE NUT BREAD

1 large loaf or 2 small loaves

1/4 c. butter, soft
1/4 c. brown sugar, packed
2 eggs
1-1/2 c. cooked wild rice
1/2 c. chopped pecans

1-1/4 c. whole wheat flour
1 tsp. baking powder
1 tsp. salt
1 tsp. nutmeg
1 tsp. cinnamon
3/4 c. milk

Cream butter and sugar; add eggs and beat until fluffy. Stir in wild rice and pecans. Stir together flour, baking powder, salt, nutmeg and cinnamon; add to creamed ingredients alternately with the milk, stirring just until dry ingredients are moistened. Grease one 3x8" loaf pan or two 3x5" pans. Pour in mixture. Bake at 325° for 55-60 minutes for large loaf, 40-45 minutes for small loaves, or until a toothpick inserted in the center comes out clean. Remove from pans and cool on wire rack.

WILD RICE AND PECAN WAFFLES

4 to 6 waffles

1 c. all-purpose flour
1 tsp. baking powder
1/4 tsp. salt
2 egg yolks
2/3 c. milk

1/4 c. vegetable oil
2 egg whites
1/2 c. chopped pecans
1 c. cooked wild rice,
   see page 8

Preheat waffle iron. Sift flour with baking powder and salt; set aside. In medium bowl, beat egg yolks, milk and oil until well-combined. Gradually add flour mixture, beating after each addition just until smooth. In small bowl, beat egg whites until stiff peaks form. Gently fold egg whites into batter just until combined. Stir in pecans and wild rice. For each waffle, pour about 1/2 cup of batter into center of lower half of waffle iron, until it spreads to 1" from edge. Cook until waffle iron stops steaming. Waffle should be golden. Serve hot.

WILD RICE BREAKFAST SCONES

Makes 8 wedges

2-1/2 c. all-purpose flour
5 Tbsp. sugar
2 tsp. baking powder
1 tsp. baking soda
1/2 tsp. salt

1/2 c. butter, cold
1 c. cooked wild rice
1/3 c. buttermilk
2 eggs
Additional sugar for top

Measure flour, sugar, baking powder, soda and salt into mixing bowl. Cut in the butter until crumbly. Mix wild rice with buttermilk and eggs; reserve a Tbsp. of the liquid. Pour remaining liquid mixture over dry ingredients. Mix just until flour is moistened; dough will be soft. Turn out onto a lightly-floured board; shape into a ball. Place on ungreased cookie sheet, roll or pat into an 8" circle. Brush with reserved egg-milk; sprinkle with sugar. With a knife, score into 8 wedges; leave in place. Bake at 400° until golden, 20-25 minutes. Remove from pan, cool on wire rack. Pull wedges apart to serve.

WILD RICE STALKS

Makes 16 stalks

1 c. cooked wild rice	1/2 c. rye flour
2 tsp. salt	3-1/2 to 4 c. bread flour
1-1/2 c. water, 105° to 115°F	Oil for cookie sheet
1 Tbsp. sugar	1 egg white, beaten with
2 packages active dry yeast	1 Tbsp. water
1/4 c. vegetable oil	Coarse salt

In bowl, combine wild rice, salt, water, sugar and yeast; let stand 5 minutes until yeast foams. Stir in oil and rye flour, add bread flour one cup at a time until mixture is stiff. Let rest 15 minutes. Turn out onto board; divide into 16 pieces. Roll each piece into a 16-20" rope; roll in oil and place on baking sheets. With scissors, snip about 1/3 of the length of each stick on both sides to resemble the grain on stalks. Brush with egg white mixture and sprinkle with salt. Bake at 375° for 20-30 minutes until browned and crisp.

WILD RICE BREADSTICKS

Makes 16 sticks

1 c. cooked wild rice,
  see page 8
2 tsp. salt
1-1/2 c. water, 105° to 115°F
1 Tbsp. sugar
2 packages active dry yeast

1/4 c. vegetable oil
4 to 4-1/2 c. all-purpose flour
Oil for cookie sheet
1 egg white, beaten with
  1 Tbsp. water
Coarse salt

In bowl, combine wild rice, salt, water, sugar and yeast. Stir to blend. Let stand 5 minutes until yeast foams. Stir in oil and flour one cup at a time until mixture is stiff. Let rest 15 minutes. Turn out onto board; divide into 16 pieces. Roll each piece of dough to make a rope 16-20" long. Roll sticks in oil and place on baking sheets. Brush with egg mixture and sprinkle with salt. Bake at 375° for 20-30 minutes until browned and crisp.

WILD RICE FENNEL SEED BREAD

Makes 4 baguettes or one "flower pot" bread

1 package active dry yeast	**2 tsp. fennel seed**
2 c. warm water, 105° to 115°F	**1-1/2 tsp. salt**
1 c. cooked wild rice	**5 to 5-1/2 c. bread flour**

In large mixing bowl dissolve yeast in the warm water. Let stand 5 minutes until yeast begins to foam. Stir in wild rice, fennel seed and salt. Add flour one cup at a time until soft dough forms, beating to keep dough satiny. When dough is too stiff to beat, cover and let stand 15 minutes. Sprinkle board with remaining flour. Knead, adding flour until dough is satiny and not sticky. Turn dough into greased bowl. Cover, let rise until doubled. Turn dough out onto lightly-oiled surface. Shape as desired according to directions below. Bake as directed. Cool on wire racks.

Baguettes: Divide dough into 4 parts. Shape each into a long, slender loaf. Place on baking pans sprinkled with cornmeal. Let rise until doubled. Brush with water; slash with sharp knife. Bake at 400°, brushing once during baking, for 20-25 minutes or until golden and crusty.

Flowerpot Bread: Shape dough into a ball. Place into a well-greased, clean clay flower pot, with the smooth side up. Let rise until doubled. Bake at 375° for 30-35 minutes or until bread tests done.

WILD RICE THREE GRAIN BREAD

Makes one large braided wreath or 3 pan loaves

2 packages active dry yeast
2-1/2 c. water, 105° to 115°F
1 c. dry milk powder
2 Tbsp. butter or lard, melted
2 tsp. salt
1/2 c. honey
1 c. uncooked rolled oats

1 c. rye flour
1 c. whole wheat flour
4 to 4-1/2 c. bread flour
2 c. cooked wild rice
1 egg, beaten with
 1 Tbsp. water
1/2 c. sunflower seeds

In large bowl, dissolve yeast in water. Add dry milk, butter, salt and honey. Stir in oats, rye flour, whole wheat flour and 2 cups bread flour to make a soft dough. Add wild rice. Let rest 15 minutes, covered. Stir in enough bread flour to make a stiff dough. Turn out onto board; knead 10 minutes. Add more flour as needed. Turn dough into bowl. (Continued)

Let rise until doubled, about 2 hours. Turn out onto floured board and divide into 3 parts.

To make round loaves: Shape into round loaves and place in greased baking pans. Let rise until almost doubled. Brush with the egg-water mixture and sprinkle with sunflower seeds. Bake at 375° for 35-40 minutes or until loaves test done.

To make a wreath: Shape each part into a strand 36" long. Braid strands together. Shape into a wreath and place on a greased baking sheet or greased 14" pizza pan. Pinch ends together. Let rise until almost doubled, about 45 minutes. Brush with egg-water mixture and sprinkle with sunflower seeds. Bake at 375° for 40-45 minutes or until the loaf tests done in the center and is well-browned.

WILD RICE HEARTH BREAD

2 loaves

1 package active dry yeast
1/3 c. warm water, 105°-115°F
2 c. milk, scalded and cooled
2 Tbsp. butter, melted
2 tsp. salt
1/4 c. dark molasses

1 Tbsp. grated orange rind
1 tsp. each: caraway seed,
  anise seed and fennel seed
2 c. whole wheat flour
1 c. cooked wild rice
4 to 4-1/2 c. bread flour

In a large bowl dissolve yeast in water. Add milk, butter, salt and molasses. Stir in orange rind, seeds and whole wheat flour. Add 2 cups bread flour; beat well. Add wild rice. Cover; let rest 15 minutes. Stir in bread flour to make a stiff dough. Knead on floured surface 10 minutes. Turn into lightly-greased bowl, cover; let rise until doubled, about 2 hours. Punch down. Divide into two parts. Place on greased pan. Let rise until almost doubled, 45 minutes. Bake at 375° 45 minutes until loaves test done.

WILD RICE CINNAMON BUTTERHORNS

Makes 32 horns

1-1/2 c. milk, scalded	1 c. cooked wild rice
1/2 c. butter	5 to 6 c. all-purpose flour
3 eggs	Soft butter
1/2 c. sugar	Cinnamon sugar
1 package yeast	1 egg beaten with 2 Tbsp. milk
1/4 c. warm water, 105°-115°F	Coarse sugar for garnish

Mix hot milk and butter, stir to melt; beat in eggs and sugar. Mix yeast and warm water in a cup, let stand 5 minutes until bubbly. Add to cooled milk mixture. Stir in wild rice and flour; beat until smooth. Cover and refrigerate overnight. Divide into 4 parts; roll each into a 12" circle. Cut each into 8 wedges. Spread with soft butter; sprinkle with cinnamon sugar. Roll up into crescents; place on greased baking sheets. Let rise until puffy. Brush with egg, sprinkle with sugar. Bake at 375° 13-15 minutes until golden.

Desserts

WILD RICE APPLE CAKE

Makes one 9x13" cake, 20 servings

1-1/3 c. brown sugar, packed
1-1/2 c. melted butter
2 eggs
1 tsp. vanilla extract
2 c. all-purpose flour
3/4 tsp. baking soda
1/2 tsp. baking powder

1 tsp. cinnamon
1/2 c. milk
2 c. chopped, pared apple
1 c. cooked wild rice,
  see page 8
1 c. chopped walnuts
1 c. raisins

Preheat oven to 350°. In large bowl, combine sugar and melted butter. Using wooden spoon, beat in eggs and vanilla. Mix flour, soda, baking powder and cinnamon; add to creamed mixture alternately with milk. Stir in apples, wild rice, walnuts and raisins. Pour into greased and floured 9x13" pan. Bake 40-45 minutes until surface springs back when gently pressed with fingertip. Let cool in pan. Frost if desired with caramel icing.

CINNAMON WILD RICE PUDDING

8 to 10 servings

3/4 c. raisins, golden or dark
1/2 c. maple syrup
2 eggs
1/2 tsp. cinnamon

1/4 tsp. nutmeg
1 tsp. vanilla
2 c. cooked wild rice
2 c. hot half-and-half
Cinnamon sugar for top

Preheat oven to 350°. Combine all ingredients and turn into a 1 1/2-quart casserole. Sprinkle with cinnamon sugar. Bake one hour or until pudding is set. Serve warm or chilled.

WILD RICE DESSERT TOPPING

Makes 4 servings

1 c. cooked wild rice
1/3 c. brown sugar

1/2 c. golden or dark raisins
1/2 c. chopped pecans

Combine all ingredients. Cover and refrigerate. Spoon mixture over vanilla ice cream, pudding or custard.

Beatrice Ojakangas is a native of northern Minnesota and has written many articles for national food magazines. She wrote a weekly newspaper column for a number of years and has authored many cookbooks, including two other books in this series, *The Best of Pancake and Waffle Recipes* and *The Best of Honey Recipes*.

Adventure
Publications
1-800-678-7006

ISBN
0-934860-56-4

ISBN 0-934860-56-4

50595>

9 780934 860567